MW00355211

I am a woman not a Winston is a collection of poetry
and photography from my heart to yours. All the
collected writings and photographs in this book were
created by C. Churchill. Who is not a man and who is
not Winston Churchill. This is my debut poetry
collection. I would like to dedicate this to my
father Jack Churchill. He threw me into the woods
and my heart has yet to leave.

My heart looks where my eyes can't see
Finding beauty lost under timid smiles
Where forgotten love discarded all hope

I see you there
I always see you

But will you ever see me?

You made me dizzy
A mixture of heart and sadness

Spinning into your dark
I forgot everything

Everything that matters
A perfect high

Let go let love
Lost in you

Breaking the broken
The sickness you bring

Hope and dreams
Last night's imagination

Your love
An uninhabitable entity

The universe
The stars

Nothing you can hold
Everything you can feel

Some say gypsy soul
I prefer escape artist

I have seen the wilds
How they capture my spirit

Every wave that crashes bringing me closer
Closer to my whole self

I don't know who I would be
If life had stuck me in a box

A woman in pieces
Perhaps a ghost

But I choose to be whole
Feeding every bit of myself

Escaping to the unknown
Whenever possible

I took a long walk
Down this old road
The one that curves left
Then right
And ultimately disappears
If only for a moment
But in that moment
Was it despair or delight?
Feeling lost
No boundaries
Exhilarating
Terrifying
My breath escaping me
Yet my eyes entranced
Partly wanting direction
Mostly needing adventure
Walking slower the further I travel
Enjoying this moment
Time was released
Dusk was coming quick
But I had no worry
My hands explored the new-found foliage
As my heart grew in bounds
My breath returned to me ten-fold
I was never really lost
My heart now found
No map was needed
To find this moment
Just a long walk
An old road
And eyes that could see
What an old soul
Desperately needs

Sex and candy

Strolling the park
A young girl's strut

Gloss in one hand
The other shaking

Not knowing her worth
Trying it all on for size

I was you long ago
I was sweet sixteen

Trying to find my place
Afraid of my own voice

Just barely living

On sex and candy

From the time, my eyes found you
I was drawn

A pull so strong
Certainly, this was kismet

My fate to be lost in your pages
Feeling everything

Like a dream
Opening a world, I burned for

I had sat with my back turned
To the chill of physical currency

Then an unarmed spark
Followed by a blaze

You lost me in you
Found me in you

A crush turned to love
Love turned to light

In my darkest days
I still grab you from the shelf

To get lost
Over and over again

Summertime rolls
Off my shoulders

Into the night
We play to muses

Sparks landing in start
Waves of passion scent the warm air

Finally sounds of laughter
Fill this garden

Among strangers smiles
Exchanged

Wander the eyes
Spreading across tables

Soul lifting gazes
Drunk on the currency of libation

Flow loosely on a melody
Dancing a quick step waltz

In tune of the grand design
Swift love to decadence

With half closed eyes, they continue
Dreaming of forgotten forevers

The snow came
As it did every spring

A fresh blanket
Over winters faded fast

Starving on remnants of wishes and want
The skeletons began to show

At first our eyes then cheeks did follow
The hunger rose to meet us

We could not contain what wasn't ours
We let this storm
Deplete us

You clipped these wings just short of flight
Pounding false promises into loves fresh bed

As I lost breath
You grew vigor

A version of love held in chains of regret
My version had only known wings

So I bit my ankles from your shackles
Free to fly with wounds still dripping

My wings beating
Covered, reaching

Reaching a place, you will never know

A place where hearts don't live in cages
A place where there is freedom to grow

TICK TOCK
TICK TOCK

The morning still
Drips linger from last night

I watch the trees filter in the day

With my cup of hope or is it sadness
Reminding me I still breathe

I have littered this path
In pieces of a broken heart

What I once thought could never be emptied
Arrived on time

I sat in wonder of the roads ahead
Taking an eternity to feel the earth

Then just as if magic entered the room
My breath caught and released

My feet began to dance
My heart began to fill

Collecting new pieces in every step
Building on what once was

And what will become

I lay motionless
Wetted by the fresh dewed grass
My heart lay beside me
I listen for the trees

The wind that rustles their leaves
Its absent

I listen for the creek nearby
The gurgling currents

I listen for the sweet sparrow song
That comes in the morning

Nothingness

When I wished I could stop feeling
I was unaware

That only in death
Could this wish come true

You broke it
That heart you longed for
Then threw it away

Such a childish way
To say
I love you

Love me in the fray
The place my heart now dwells

My broken parts
Sorted and manageable
I know the fray is messy
Love is always a risk

So, love me in the fray

Where past is present and present is past
Where we don't hide what we are made of
Because it was where we learned to be strong
Where we learned to love
Love with all the consequences

So, love me in the fray

Where broken are the words not the people
Because no one escapes war torn edges
Threads unravel
Frayed and beautiful
Life touches us all

Now love me in the fray
where love is as real as it gets

I remember the first morning I woke
To all the sights and sounds
I had only been dreaming

The veil had been dissolved within tears shed
My heart met the sky in wonder again

My eyes ready to take it all in
Into my heart the winds crept

Not the darkness that had become my friend
I felt all those things differently now

I felt

That's when I knew I had survived

I kept searching for someone to understand
See my mess for what it was
An intricate web of survival

Chaotic it seemed to most
The way my heart bleeds

Splatters on the mirror
I no longer see

They collected every drop
As I ran out of fingers
Then out of toes

Counting on losses
And friends turning foes

All the while they took and took
My splatters
My tears

Comfort in knowing they had nothing to fear
Lightning doesn't strike twice you see

Keep me close
They are free
Free of the blood
Free of the tears

I was the crime scene
They just brought the beer

We flew in circles
looking into the sun

Never realizing
what we had done

Locking ourselves in
to something so maddening

Where windows were dirty
with last night's sadness

We fly in circles
till our last breath

Caught
Suffocating

The sun can't save us
we are beyond gravity

Holding onto nothing
except our insanity

Embrace this storm my love
You are so close

Hold onto your tomorrow
Feel inside of it

Where you can find peace amongst chaos
Where you can make sense

Where ego and stubbornness have left
There is only room for strength for truth for love

Leave those others they are not necessary
For this storm was created by you

And is only brought by fear
It will subside

When it is no longer being fed

Demons come
Demons go

Sleight of hand robs your soul

Let them come
Steal your love

Beg them to play your mind above

Sleight of hand
Slight of heart

Escape is futile
When you have fallen apart

Heal those breaks
Before you step

Be one last person
Who lost respect

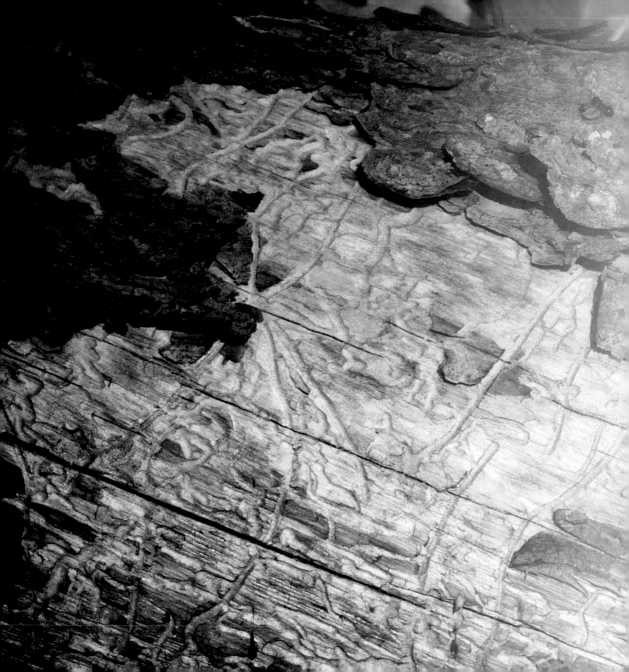

My love it's not simply

about

the

breaking

But how we arrange the pieces

That's the beauty

Those cries we hear in the middle of the night
The ones filled with desperate and longing

Lay them upon your pillow

Sleep

They will not break the morning
If they call within the day

Pull them close
Its ok

Let them know they have a voice
Set them free

That's all they ever wanted

I want to write of the moon
And how the glow complimented the stars in your eyes
But that is all common sense

Let's talk about the moldy bagels in the kitchen
Or the dishes in the sink
The things I just smiled at

Because I know life is hard
I know what it is like to be suffocated
Alone

Let's talk about the cat puke I almost stepped in
When you had no time to clean
If you wish we could connect with the stars and the sea
Speaking to how you encapsulated me

Or we could talk about how you devastated my heart
For not understanding
For not seeing you
We could talk about that

Or we could not waste breath
Because I saw you
The one you hide
And I accepted every bit of it

But I was the broken one
The one you had to walk away from

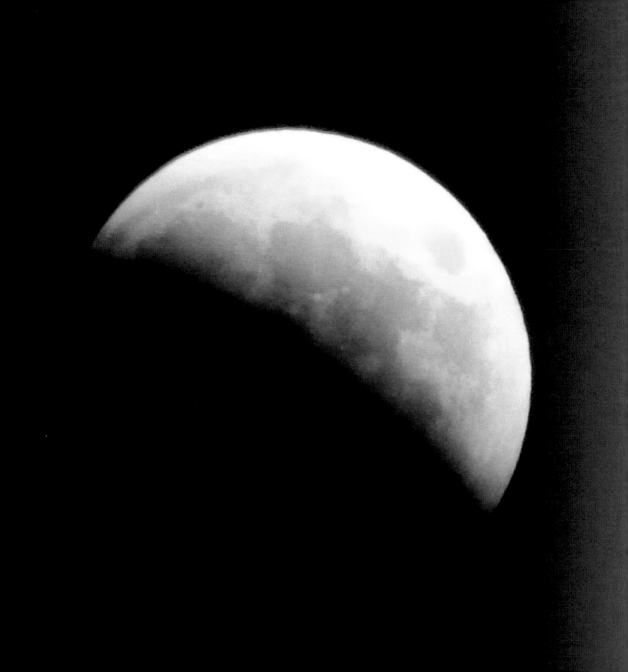

There will come a time
When there is nothing left to say

When it doesn't matter if I go
or if I stay

If I get this feeling
that is where this train is headed

I will go silent

When the last hope has lost its voice
And the endgame is near

In this silence
Don't try to find me

I have already
disappeared

I have these shoes
I buy them every year

Converse low tops
All Stars

I am not sure when it started
But it's always for my birthday

Maybe when I was seventeen
The colors they change

I still love the black
Going back for those every so often

There is something about this shoe
I can't quite put my finger on

Sure, they are cool
Timeless even

But not completely comfortable
Nor do they last
But I buy them every year
The only thing that doesn't change

Maybe I need these shoes
In order to remain

The tune echoes in the lonely parts
the ones I no longer show

Saving the melody of secrets
under my brow

I tried to share with wild eyes
open and ready

I couldn't keep them open
They ache now and again
They ache for you

A you I can't retrieve
A you I can't recreate
A you I lost before becoming me

Not sure if the new me is happy or sad
I know she is alive
I know she is here

Somedays hungry
Somedays craving the music of yesterday

For my Midwestern girls
rum runners placed on knees knees
they could not reach
Get me a beer sweetheart
with a lingering hand
The sun was bright on the lake
pontoons and speedboats

Everybody's escape

Poor we were with our forts freshly made
of Sunday sheets
and our everything eaten was always beef
Dad hunting out back while the world was laid off
It might have been squirrel or rabbit who knows
But we lived on the lake

Everybody's escape

Staring at stars just hoping to get away
Everybody normal everybody fine
Front yard beatings laced in cocaine lines
hidden corners everywhere filled with abandon

Everybody's escape

Children placed s pawns for dreams crushed
the blame Oh the blame

That's why he hit me
That's why I stayed
For you kids

Maybe just the times
Maybe the factories bleeding everyone dry
Maybe these Midwestern girls learned to spit fire instead of cry
If you see one you will know they never let hands get too close

I guard certain places more than others
Certain places deep inside

I am complicated
A natural disaster

But I know about love
and I know it doesn't play hurtful games

It tends like a garden
It soothes like rain

Burning fires for infinity
Lighting the darkest nights

It does not take a heart and splay it wide
Picking apart the very insides

I let that happen
Let the trespasser by

Learning a lesson
erring on the cautious side

You took me at my worst
Putty in your hands

Savoring each sliver
Of my waning confidence

Blind for so long
Under your cold grasp

Finally teaching myself to see
Past the past

Now adjusted to my own two feet
My head high and eyes wide

My heart begins to beat
One last glance and I am free

Walking right past your shallow
Into my deep

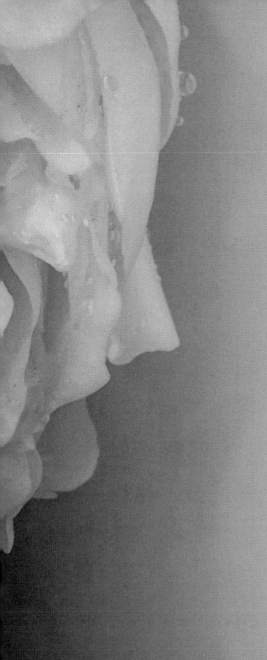

Petals soft
In rains still coming

Storms they rage under and over
again
Puddles of tears
Escaping into rivers of passion

Flow
Deep

Currents leading
Where hearts stand bleeding

Pull my petals
Till I am bare
Pull them soft

One by one
He loves me he loves me not

Till I am empty

They speak to me
These battle worn timbers
Of days gone by

Attracted to the soul of a place
I am drawn
Wandering the desolate

There I find peace
In the broken
In the heart

In the silence
There I find myself

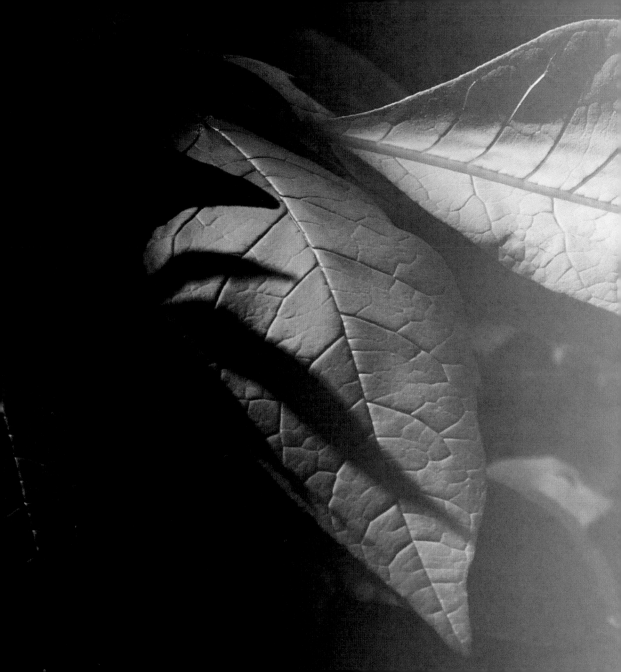

So, I was throwing ideas like carrots in a pot
Wondering if the world will enjoy this book I am making

It may be a bit bizarre
Or maybe they will be enamored in the write way

Maybe snow falls heavy on their hearts as it has mine

I wonder and wonder even more
As keys strike me deep

It's kind of scary this writing thing
Letting it all out then searching for more

A poem, a line, a verse, I am hooked
Hard to say when it will end

Because there are words
I have yet to find

Hold me close
This fog is greedy

A moment of blindness
Could lose me forever

Hammered pavement
Where chalk hearts lie

Breaking chunks into pieces
Then shatters

This chest broken deep
Where does it hurt the most?

Break my arm
Break my stride

They heal
They know their purpose

But what of hearts
Just a fraction of life

The beat familiar
One two

Hold tight for the breaking

Yes, you will live
Yes, you will breathe

And one day your heart will ask
Can we do this again?

I stop when you get me high

This path is forbidden
It always has been

They always want to go deeper
Deeper than the one before

But baby
My deep will knock you silly

Then you will treat me as a child
Just wading in

When I am clearly a woman

Who has survived

Oceans of shipwrecks

Winters drippings collect in pools
Like liquid dreams

As the green unfurls another spring
How do we see past?

Each year growing older
Time disappears

My height stays the same
No longer growing on the scale of youth

Keeping it all in my mind
And in my heart, you see

Growing in ways
My young self couldn't dream

Our eyes hold tight to this youth
In aging cracks of fantasy

Where we had chances, we came
Brought our finest

But the world keeps moving on
Through our bodies through our minds

We race to the end
Even faster now

Love me harder
Love me deeper

Shatter upon me
A blanket of stars

An impact so great

I am no longer
Afraid of the dark

Can we meet here
Halfway between love and insanity?

That's what hearts do
Living on the edge of it all

Give me your hand
Let's jump together

There would be nothing worse
Than falling alone

She lost herself in this magic

Smitten by hope

That love still flowed

In these veins

I love the feeling of your eyes
Washing over me
They lay me down like prey
As I quickly catch your gaze
Fingers begin the trace
Up my inhibitions you climb
Reaching through me
Down my spine

The chills reek of fear and sweetness
Just short of blinding madness

You take your time
Your sweet beautiful time

You took my heart
Looked deep into the cracks

I was waiting
Waiting for you to run

Instead you looked into my eyes and smiled

You said that one looks like mine
That was all I ever needed to fall in love

My shadow lay patient
Across the sun
Under the moon

It's there
Beneath yours
While our darkness bleeds

Lovers amidst raw truth
We echo infinity

Tears on lashes
Begin the frost

Frozen between snowflakes
In shadows lost

A slumber known
As winters kiss

Are but tears
Of those we miss

When I can't find my breath
Then it was real

The fear shaking me in the night
That secret sister life

Where the darkness reigns
Coming to haunt the light in me again

Lives running parallel
Always on empty

Building walls to save our hearts
Or is it our souls we strive to protect

Bleeding hearts heal just fine
But what of a broken mind

One day we all wake
Realizing we have been doing it wrong
Realizing the sun still comes
That's when we start to dig
Digging past the skeletons
Trying to unearth the secret to why
Digging further
Further than we have been
That's where we find the nothing
The deep vast silence
As we scream into the nothing
Beyond the light of sanity

We wait
Waiting for answers
Waiting for that miniscule echo

To tell us we were right all along
Only silence returns our plea

That's when we wake
That's when we realize

There is no such thing as why

On this island, I remain

A gun in one hand

A shovel in the other

Always choosing the slow death

There is another funeral today

I sat with my coffee under the morning sun
Breathing last night's cigarette

Slowly they pull in
Dressed in black

Eighty-four degrees and rising

There is always a mixture
Of hellos and goodbyes
Of laughter and tears

A collection of emotions
A donation for the pine box

A box that sits
Waiting for eternity

Between a shed tear and a passing smile
I grab a warm up
Light a cigarette

There was another funeral today

I miss hearing I am beautiful
I miss being sought by wanton eyes
I miss being adored
And I miss being counted

At the end of everyday
Crying for touch
Crumpled into myself
The night unforgiving

Realizing I am the woman
I never thought I would be
Begging for any kind of love
On the corner of desperate and lonely

This glass is filled with moments yet to come
Laced intoxicating dreams

Chilled glass potions
A lost souls dance to wash it all down
Sweet divinity
Between the church and the corner

Cheers to the day drinkers
Coated in backward glances
While the storms come heavy
The conversations stay light
And they are always at the end
Before the beginning of the night

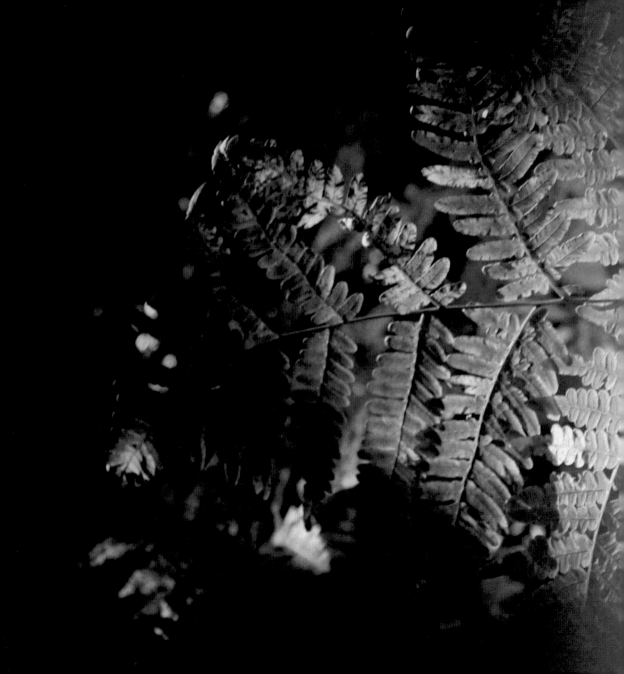

Slate grey skies consumed this view
My hands lost on stagnant winds

Screaming
Drowning

As chilled waters fill empty spaces

Connected
Suffocating

All direction lost

Where is North?
Where is South?

When pain is blinding

I drop six feet
Into the ready earth
How it beckons me

Fires below
First to indulge

Burning
Consumed

I disappear

I found peace in this darkness

Where I used to cry

Where I used to scream

I took it all
All the world had given me

Laid it out on the sands of time
Watched it shine and change in the light

Every grain a memory
Building a ship instead of a wall

Looking towards the journey
A love no longer lost

I took the blooms
The ones that broke free

Free from this full heart
And placed a crown upon my head

Holding it in a way
That moved forward instead of against

Ready
Ready for anything to come

I became a woman

Not when my first period came
Not when I gave myself for the first time
Not when the first man treated me like an object

I became a woman

When I saw my value
When I saw that my body didn't matter
But my mind was the key

I became a woman

When I could look upon other women with a kind heart
Instead of jealousy

I became a woman

It took a very long time
I had to shed the ideas everyone put before me

I became a woman

When I realized
Being a woman was seeing me for me
And not giving a shit what everyone else sees

Healing takes time
Pots of strong coffee
Cases of cold beer
Packs of cigarettes
Sleepless nights
Tear soaked pillows

Healing takes time

Lost loves
Kisses wasted
Dark corners
Steps misplaced

Healing takes time
Nightmares during the day
Anxious filled breaths
Confidence on the back burner

Healing takes time
Mistakes are made

Promises broken
Words left unsaid

Healing takes time
But the journey is yours
Take it in stride

You will fly again

I just wanted to say thank you to everyone who has supported
me in my life journey. It has been a wild ride for sure.
Sometimes I have taken the path and sometimes the path has
taken me.
I am so very happy it led me here. I have had the pleasure
of meeting some of the most amazing souls on this earth.
I mean amazing amazing. If you are reading this, chances
are you belong to this incredible tribe.
A tribe of survivors, visionaries, dreamers and lovers.
A hope you enjoyed this glimpse into my writing and
photography
All my photos were shot here in my home state of Michigan.
So, come visit already. I enjoyed this process very much and
as always. Looking forward to the next adventure!

Keep dreaming my friends, xoxoxo Cheryl

About the Author:

Hello everyone, let's see what's pertinent information? I am currently pursuing my Master's Degree. I have been writing forever and taking photos even longer. I love creating and my living room looks like Martha Stewarts crazy half-sister lives in it. I grew up in a small town in Michigan. I run in the woods with no inhibition,

In a nutshell, I am an adventurer and artist. This is my first book that has seen the light of day

I am pretty sure it will be ridiculed by the scholars in writing circles and I am fine with that. You can find me chasing the sun or on Facebook.com/cchurchillwrites and Instagram @cc_writes.